Jenny Seibicke
blue fifteen

AF190999

Jenny Seibicke

blue fifteen

poetry pieces

Bibliografische Information der Deutschen Nationalbibliothek:
Die Deutsche Nationalbibliothek verzeichnet diese
Publikation in der Deutschen Nationalbibliografie; detaillierte
bibliografische Daten sind im Internet über http://dnb.dnb.de
abrufbar.

Verlag: BoD · Books on Demand GmbH, In de Tarpen 42,
22848 Norderstedt

Druck: Libri Plureos GmbH, Friedensallee 273, 22763
Hamburg

ISBN: 978-3-7597-3407-5

INSIDE THE SHELL

Inside my shell, inside my shell
I can breathe and live as well
Stars do wander over skies
I don't need to close my eyes

Nowhere else so safe and warm
Inside no harm, inside no harm
May the waves still rush ashore
I don't feel them anymore

Shimmering treasure is all mine
Sleeping beauty breaks my spine
Doesn't matter, doesn't matter
Secretly I like to shatter

The silence is so peaceful here
No one listens to a tear
Trembling in a violet shell
No one to tell, no one to tell

RAINBOW

The pages turn, the sunspots burn
In silence rainbows settle
Nights are cold and grief takes hold
Since it's a forced battle

My tongue tastes bitter, flowers they wither
Back then I froze in gaze
Once in a while, sometimes a smile
In likeness' sullen daze

INVINCIBLE

Why build a circle of defence around
The thing inside is not to be bound
Eventually changing the rules of a fight
Will never give back the previous might
Build a wall with the heaviest stones
It'll crumble and fall and break your bones
Run into the woods, hide in a tree
Flames will lick and ashes will be

L O S E R

Dazed, dreamless and not aware
Hands reaching out into the air
Trembling, restless, pale like the moon
Who is going to sleep far too soon

In the cold light of morn
New senses are born
Crows are crying, birds don't sing
Unbreakable chains are what they bring

Woken up, confused yet aware
I know I can't feel what isn't there
Helpless, struggling, it'll stay the same
I'm the loser of my one-man-game

UNDER A DIFFERENT MOON

While rain is falling endlessly
Running days come close to be
One in a shade, one in the mist
I am hunted by waterblue fist

Why don't I move, I am the prey
Back and forth my feet do sway
Not prepared to leave my shell
Yet there's nothing more to tell

Hours pass disappointingly
Lips do part with whispered she -
Farewell now, goodbye is soon
Maybe under a different moon

XIBALBA

On your roots, Xibalba,
my weary hands find rest
and the blushing edges
of my consciousness are fed
the overpowering
pulse of earth

they bleed no more
and no more are
narrow senses mine
but a blur of
autumn breathing whistles

my spine has freed
its wavelike sculpture,
Xibalba, for it flows,
a mighty vein of yours,
stemlike into
golden leaves and
up the air beyond

against your
woodsmell bark
I press my cheek
and, Xibalba,
for too short a minute

the mind within escapes
the sticky webs of
ever darkening reality

silent friend
your tale is more
than words
Xibalba
out of reach
your source
of eternity

AS SIMPLE AS THAT

It's the absence of
the reassuring blinking
of that little digital
letter on my mobile
phone after a day
of distress

sometimes it's as
simple as that

when the emptiness
of an electronic mailbox
brings tears to my
sleep-deprived eyes
and the page
remains blank

it can seem
so trivial

but also real life's
well-kept tragedies:
a heavy-headed
semi-creative
drowsiness caused
by too much

cheap red wine
many solitary
nights and
fags I can't
give up - it most
readily creates
the illusion of
leading a life
in troubled
modesty as long
as not pondered
upon

the stories untold
the places unlived in
shimmering in irreal
translucency and the
promise of a chance
the yearning of
outrageous loneliness
for completion, the
love still to be found
maybe to be found
in days to come
most likely not
even beyond that
point, we knew
that the odds were
against us

we took it to the next level
we always did

I still remember
our shared fascination
for the unnoticed:
the haunting beauty
of a greyish tree trunk
or the soft skin on the
bare neck of a woman
one row ahead

and the hopelessness
behind it all,
after all

I was never alone

YOU AT THE PIANO

Something about
you at the piano -
your long nails
clicking keys
before the sound
pre-melodious

And your hair
carelessly tied
in a rebellious knot
Dark straw,
the back of
your head

A lioness' eyes
roaring in laughter

FORGET-ME-NOTS

You see,
nothing's changed
they bury
their dead
like they did
the same words,
another tongue
what does it matter?
what is it all?

See the ivy
creep its way
through the
earthly remnants
of forever
and primroses

Between the stones
among the roots -
they cling to
the marble
in comfort -
I find the
light of
a yearning blue

the colour
of your eyes
in despair

I find a bunch of
forget-me-nots
I gaze at them
as if in a dream

I find a bunch of
forget-me-nots
and struggle for
trespass in vain

SCENT OF HAPPINESS

This is the
perfect scent
of happiness
rising from
green grass
dangling from
spring buds
intruding the
air beyond

Never set down
on the rooftops
never settle
before the unknown

Always remember
life is upon you
regardless
the morning
to come

INFIDELITY

Given the chance
I'd find it -
you'd still
be there
I need to
admit my
infidelity
to high hopes
and dreamscores:
your imperfect
shade, hardly
a match for
my neurosis
dances on my
brow whenever
my mind
grows inattentive
and lashes
are shut to
the world

Is it the lack
of replacement?
for I can't
see why
I'm evoking
this pain-stained
memory

I have to admit
my infidelity
this much I
owe to myself

ABORTIVE EXORCISM

not evoking the tainted
memory of new moon's
blasphemous nights
yet feeling the urge
of being haunted by
that ghost of your
cheeky perfection
so random from the
truth of my yearning
it makes me wonder
incessantly blushing
when you lay your
blueish eyes on me
I may have missed
the exit lights whilst
they were still on
now departure is
not granted anymore
since hesitation
feels deliberate

how is it that
whenever I'm
down it's your
embrace that
lures me, seems

to be as close
to home as it
can get so that
intoxicated, nearly
brain-dead, I
seek your arms
like salvation

what am I actually
looking for when
I'm lying my -
crying my way
into your chest
entering the
sentiment proof
skin of your
shellfishy being

I want to rip
you open, discover
you to be human
behind all this
defensive carelessness,
your carnivorous
hedonism
that suits you
so well

oh how I long
to rest my head

on your velvety
heart which I know
is afraid of beating
run your resolute
hand once more
through the

contemplative whirls
of my dishevelled
hair, confuse me
linger on
the back of my
nervous head,
it's my favourite
place, I know you
can be tender

you say you'd like
me too much, that
I'm far
too important to...
you'd dead break me
and I believe you,
so why this challenging
of given reality
again and again
like it was just some
tenacious
modelling clay
ready to filter my

wishes after the
millionth imprint
of this both teary
and stubborn
nonsense of mine

sometimes I'm
indifferent to the
possibility of losing
you I wonder
if these moments
are closer to
the truth
than those in which
I think you my life

KUOLLUT

Name the devil
among the grave
Bind it in words
and you'll be safe

but yet...
and still...

Strangle the ghost
with deafening words
you grow stronger
the more it hurts

and still...
no more...

dead
mort
tot
muerto
kuollut
morto

Poetry
just a feather
against the storm
Speechless

GOODBYE LONDON!

I leave you
bereft of a home
returning home
with yet another
strapped to my back
an everlasting
stowaway
to declare

My fingers
tasted the piano
catching greyish
splinters as I stroked
the bark of some
fat bellied oak
on the Heath

Looking down
on your lights,
those lights
beckoning me,
as your breath
grows paler
urging me to dive
into your veins

down to Trafalgar's
buzzing streets

And the river,
your heart,
carries my soul
to the sea
shrieking gulls
hunting bats
through parks
of despair
through gardens
of delight

Remember me
for I won't be long
and when day
touches night,
gently,
I'll return
with my
sorrowful heart
laughing

UNDEFEATED

Yes,
there still is
a spark
ignition needs
only a look
of completed
apprehension
a ghost, that is

flames to the core
and I blaze higher
soaring skin
and I burn free

no need for
further
appreciation
beyond the
embers
nothing
remains

I am fooled
no longer
I'll end like
a torch

disused
and that's it

there'll be
no sealing it
I know
even before -
yet you turn
and I smile
stubbornly
glowing
undefeated

DECLARATION OF INDEPENDENCE

From now on no glance
shall ever keep me from
celebrating the freedom
of a life ruled by
self-sufficiency and denial.

From now on my feet
shall walk their path
never caring for the
painful acceleration
of a heart in breaking.

From now on the world
shall be mine
for the taking
I reign, am reigned
by my ignorance alone.

Only once in a while
my wandering mind
shall stop in flight
confirming what I
need not know:
I am but lonely.

DARKNESS

Darkness is all-encompassing
lithium in my veins and the
constant dragging down
towards seashells and silence

I will never be lifted

light
light is an illusion for
the subconsciously blinded
elite of hope

for I live in shadows
so dressed up in
despair I can't stand
the nakedness of
my silhouette against
the bleaching of
a new dawn

I have to run
now is never
and the empty
slopes of tomorrow
will soon weep

with blood I
never shed

or did I, did I
bleed for a
thousand causes
outside my
inconsolable self
and the pins
driven within
the whimpering
heart of mine

I can't seem
to unravel
the intermingling
tendencies of
self-destruction
and pain

it simply
doesn't matter
mine is the
seaweed and
the octopus'
kiss on the scar
a woolfian
loss, I am sure

for my bones
are as heavy as
legions of ruby
uncut

NIGHTMARE

I woke to the sound of
my heart breaking
my chest splitting open
in a final attempt
to escape into semi-
darkness which long
lost its proportion
to the touchable
night sky already
bleaching when I lay
there struggling to
breathe in what is
and is not real

please don't touch
this nightmare it
may turn on me
tearing its claws
into my white
devoted flesh
exposed since
I've found out you
can hurt me in
my dreams just
imagine the day
when -

BE GONE

So be it.
queen of heart
you've never
wanted to be
crowned with
laurels, victory
over my strange
adhesion

just an ace
up the sleeve
just the in-case
weapon in a
yet unbattled field
all I want of
you now is
passive attraction

you'd owe me
a fey escape-rope
after years of
silent admonishing
and sending-off
intimate grounds

the game's on
I've lost you
so many times

there still is
a high score
to beat

so be it.
be gone.

ROOTS OF WORSHIP

Entangled
in the roots
of worship
I remain
untouched

MODERN TIMES

We've had enough

Look at the world:
a gigantic nest
of mechanical creation
ready to overwhelm
what sense we have left

Yes, humankind
has conquered
and humankind
has spread
its glorious vision
of white manhood
among the savage
hiding in the bushes
among the pagan
praising the moon

Hail to the potent,
blind leaders -
get to the shovels!
let's celebrate some
raging victory
by digging
new mass graves

unparalleled in history
but, for unity's sake,
beware of tombstones!
- these evil reminders
indicating identity -
an inapt thing
which long is
deemed to be
silly dreamer's
mere illusion

How long have we been
entangled in the glittering
net of shiny machinery,
some mass-produced idols
slowly choking all
that we are and
all that is: life!
Unique.
Manifold.
Sacred.

But through
deceptive filters
of modern media
we perceive the
world as a
playground
righteously
manipulated

by those
undenied rulers
justified by
their hybris alone

A progress
built on the
suffocation of
the weak is
no acquisition
This mechanical
apathy will
lead us down
the metallic
path of
self-destruction

Change will not come
over those asleep
Wake up!
It's time we
reinvent ourselves

DERANGED

Why, at night,
what life doesn't
grant me?
You and your
volatile closeness
vanish with
morning's triumphant
army of sunrays
day after day
again and again

And I can't sleep
anymore, afraid
subconscious
memories of
neverbeen
gather forces
for conquest
I can't stand
the sight of
these even planes
of hopelessness
at hand

Your marble-eyes
follow me
unlooking
My deranged dream
knows the future
it will never have

Tell me then
what should I
look for?

I'm lonely

Your nocturnal
visits are the only
image my soul bears
scarred, blessed
self-defiant
towards what is
now and was and
ever will be

WHAT I MADE YOU

It isn't that hard
to admit, is it?
For it becomes
the helpless tragedy
my life obviously
needs to be

well then, let's face it
you're the only muse
roaming my depths
like an undead even
after being shot
in the head
repeatedly

clearly it's not you
but my lyrical arabesques
are fed by the
essence of what
I made you

I can't seem to
find the will to
let you slip into
semi-darkness
of memory gone

44

until someone else
pops into my
blurred vision

still, I lost the tingling
comfort of drowning
into another's eyes
I can't breathe no
more outside myself
since I ran out of
glue to fix the pieces
with you

L I E

Roam the world
beyond the leaves
of homegrown oaks
beneath the crown
of sycamores in
bench dotted parks
where doves won't rest

Dive the city's
fastest lane into
the core of today's
fancy hot spot
feel the dream
dressed in future's
glittering uncertainty -

Oh London,
you're not salvation
you're just a mood
of velvety clouds
slowly sinking in
purple goodbyes
a diversion for
the messed -up
and torn apart

Find me,
I'm all dressed
up and I
break with laughter
into shatters all
over the sky
but I'm a liar

Self-defence
is wearing me down
to piles of
personalized rags
my soul wears
in defiance
as it cares not
to rise for
a ghost

C O L O U R S

read me my colours
I never knew that
I existed outside
the blackness which
has swallowed too
many suns before
you came along
searching my twisted
heart's capsula
with eyes like rays
of light caressing
what was left on
the brink of destruction

I want to lie
entangled in your
hair, the colour
of sunset, twirls
around my dreamtips
like a promise
I sink into your
presence calmly,
sheltered from
battering forces
of days on end
a refugee in bliss

unfold me, I need
to find me without
myself in a moment
of pure presence
I need to be told
my story anew

your skin is enough
for a lifetime
of poetry
written on your
cheek, breathless
I discover the
one thing I know

your fragrance
follows my every
gesture, the air
is my witness
I'm falling for you

DESPAIR

Black straws
kissing the bottom
of glasses
Bachmann would know
the despair
you don't
you're gone
gone are the days
stretched to
their limits
nights without end
gone

How I'd love
to dive again
into the impossible
gone
you are gone
gone the despair

MORE THAN HUMAN

.

Close your mouth
she said as I
stood with
my black coal
chimney throat
gaping wide
trying to
catch luminescent
droplets
to cover the burn
inhale the wet
from the sky
but no, she said
'tis not the
greens
only dirt
from the tube
drains and warehouses
and cars and
people and people
and people
their skins
falling off
strands of hair
little reminders
turning to dust

and I rinsed
my tongue with
a gulp of
gold spirit
and clenched
my fist
for the hunger
is still there

And I stared
and I lingered
in front
of a bookshop
and I stared
and I wondered
and watched
for a leaf

come on, she urged
and pulled at
my backpack
come on, she pulled
they're waiting
let's go

I turned back
and fell in
beside her
not looking
strode down

the pavement
while seagulls
they cried

Oh am I not human
what am I but human
I am more than human
and I long for the sea

L O S T

Midnight escapes me
meridian is lost
out of sight
screws and timbers
holding
holding
...
still
reality still
fast and strong
what I'd give
for a flight
what I'd give
for a dream
before spring

DECADE-DANCE

You: fleeting as ever
prone to embrace
any attraction readily
but my outstretched
heartbeat

Are you still
prowling the streets
purring, ready to
jump on your
mesmerized victim –
but I don't
know you anymore

Perhaps I never did
mistaking your
affection for care
parading tenderness
in broad daylight
but was it?
I'll never know now
if you retreat
to the undergrowth
sprung from fear
of losing control

or was it meant as a
coup de grace
born out of pity?
Regardless
You disappeared
behind the scenes

But did you?
In your decade-dance
swirling through
nights, extending
your grasp into
fresh ground
as if to make sure
I am still yours
But was I?

AUTUMN'S CURSE

autumn always wins
a slow undressing
of the world
bared bones for
winters gnawing breath
frost is not
an option yet
it's not sudden
it's not brutal
peeling off
the colours
as if it is for love
autumn's curse
we won't remember
until spring

A L I V E

Parallel lives unfold
as I am running in circles
the world has shrunk
crushing me
while I'm expanding

maybe that my hair
gets entangled into
strings of kelp, cold
in the nape of my neck
my toes tickled
by sun-kissed pebbles
on some remote beach
meaning I am
still here
making me feel
Alive

WELL PAST

Life's but a web
of entangled knots
decisions not made
for fear of truth

if there is comfort
in the known
I'm well past feeling it
if there is imbalance
in yearning
I'm well past knowing it

THE SEA

oh how I long for the sea
always ahead of me
always ahead of me

in dreams I am
filled to the brim
with the blue
that never sees day

always ahead of me
oh how I long for
how I long for the sea

waking up breathless
a bit less each day
leaving behind a
dripping trail of myself
pouring out my heart
until it trips on with a sigh

oh how I long for the sea

YESTERYEAR

meet me back
in the shadows
of yesteryear
where a whisper
meant anything
a ghost
a tree
a kiss

deep in the forest
in the tangle of roots
the pond never was
quiet
never lay
still
always mirroring
infinity

here's a guess:
life happened
not by surprise
but slowly
creeping up on me
a stealthy choker
drenching my thirst

before I realized

I long for

the sea

THE BOTTOM

Get to the bottom of
your own unhappiness
easier said than done
the glass is half-full,
as goes the saying,
but I'm bumping my head
trying to dive for
hidden treasures

nothing's more obscure
than your own desires
always dressing in negations

SUDENKORENTO

Those days are past
A new dawn already
Eager to fill their place
The void between
That's you. That's now.
Take a breath.
Here.
Now.
Gone.

We take everything
For granted
The tomorrow
That may never come
The hardest thing:
To just BE

I wish I was a cat
Basking in the glory
Of the sun
Caring for nothing
But the warmth on its fur

OCEANSOUL

I am made of water and salt

my bones branch
like ancient corals
reaching for the sun
my blood boils
like thunderous waves
crashing on black stone
born in fire, moulded in ice
roaring through a heart
too blue to sleep
and my mind…
a never-ending sirens' song
luring the sea
into my pores
wailing until the
coastal wind
catches my cry

I'm home once
my pebbly toes
merge with the sand
and I can breathe
no more

FEATHER

I do love you
but I'm not on fire

my love is as tender
as the ruffled breast feathers
of a bird in spring
warming, caressing
but not taking flight

I wish it was both
comfort, cover
and escape to
dizzying heights
lightheaded soaring
to get us out of here

not sure if it can
grow wings
and secure
us a nest
I'm not sure
if it can do both

I'm not sure

ON WHICH THE SUN DOESN'T RISE

hush
late gets the night
hush now and let me
blue are the shadows
that dance to reveal
blue is the ocean
that rises to meet
my heart, my desire
my heart's desire
hush now let me
late gets the night
hush now let me
breathe

hush now
for no one's ears is that
on which the sun doesn't rise

WHERE THE SLEEPING MEET THE DEAD

A dramatic poem

I

Very dark when the audience enters, orchestral music playing loudly, suddenly stops when everyone is seated. Silence for a while. Black. The poem is read by a small child in a white dress, who appears on stage like a ghost. An air of mystery and oddness is being created. The last stanza is repeated, slowly fading out. Dim lights switch on.

Asleep we're born
Asleep we'll die
We'll bear the scorn
We will defy

We march, we breed
We grow, we feed
We hurt, we bleed
We'll reap the seed

Call it a dream
Take it for real
Say what you deem
Do what you feel

Truth is obscure
There is no cure
Fall for the lure
You'll endure

Endless day
Endless night
We will stay
We will fight

Asleep we're born
Asleep we'll die
We're the 'lorn
Unanswered cry

Asleep we're born
Asleep we'll die
Cease to wonder
There is no why

II

An imaginary space. Two genderless people, Jamie and Alex. They are put here by nobody and without knowing why. They're caught up in their minds. They note the surroundings, but they don't care: A small, square room that opens to the audience. Walls are made of grey concrete; one has a single-coloured graffiti on it. Lights are dim, there is no ceiling. Outside the room, a tree in bloom, people passing from time to time, chatting and laughing. Each scene is followed by a black.

The characters constantly switch from surges of emotion to completely calm, unmoved reflection. These changes always happen abruptly. Half of the time, the characters enter dialogue, the other half they soliloquize. Sometimes their monologues mix and complement each other.

Jamie and Alex are standing in the middle of the room, back-to-back, spinning round simultaneously. They inspect the room turn to face each other. Their faces remain blank. This goes on for a long moment, at the point when the audience starts to get uneasy, Jamie speaks.

J: *as if already in the middle of a conversation*
          The problem is: am I awake, am I not?

A: Who knows?
          turns away and stands facing the wall, unanimated throughout the scene

J: *helpless gesture*
          I don't.

70

A: Someone does.

J: I don't know who does.

A: *sitting, back against the wall*
       Someone must.

J: And how should I know if the one who knows
       really knows?

A: You can't.

J: *bitter*
       Trusting someone before trusting myself.

A: You must.

J: *starts pacing the little space*
       Let's say I'm asleep.

A: We don't know that.

J: If I am -

A: If we are...

J: If we are, we shouldn't move.

A: Shouldn't talk.

J: Shouldn't even think!

A: *watching the pacing, ironically*
        Sleepwalking is dangerous.

J: You don't feel it when you fall.

A: And you will sleep forever, not because you didn't
        wake up but because you are dead already.

J: *stops for a moment*
        Dead already.

A: Are we?

J: *ignoring the question*
        Suppose we are awake.

A: You are awake.

J: Then what?

A: Change.

J: From what to what?

A: *annoyed*
        Above all: why?

J: *reads out the graffiti on the wall*
Life is nothing but transformation. Life is nothing but transformation. Life is nothing but transformation. Life is nothing but transformation. Life is nothing but transformation. Life is nothing but transformation. Life is nothing <u>without</u> transformation.

A: *stands up to read the graffiti, shrugging*
So it's nothing.

J: That's something.

A: And what exactly is it?

J: Nothing.

A: Well, you have to start from somewhere.

J: *desperate*
So nothing? If you start from nothing, you'll get to nothing, through nothing cause there's nothing to be had from nothing.

A: So transformation is nothing, too.

J: *bangs their head against the wall with the graffiti*
I need to know if I'm asleep. I need to know if I'm asleep!

A: *watches intently*
Does it help?

J: *already bleeding, stops*
Doesn't seem like it does.

A: *does the same on the opposite wall*
Am I awake, am I awake, am I awake?

J: Does it help?

A: *keeps on bumping their head into the wall*
Am I awake am I awake?

J: *suddenly addressing the audience*
What if hitting my head is part of a dream, in which I try to find out if I sleep? Can't I only wake into another dream then?

A: *weakly*
Am I awake?

J: What if you are so awake, bumping your head won't change a thing?

They turn to face each other like in the beginning.

A: But if I am awake...

J: and I am asleep...

A: how is it possible...?

J: we meet?

They stare, then turn away.

A: Maybe it's not.

J: *still agitated*
        But it is.

A: It's nothing, remember?

Sitting down again.

J: Still it is.

A: A dream to me?

J: Real for me?

A: Who knows?

J: Anyone.

A: No one.

J: Someone.

A: We can't trust.

J: No.

III

In the background, the sound of a heart beating unevenly, accelerating till the end of speech.

J: *addressing the audience, battered*
        So here I am. Guess I got rejected, violently beaten down by someone's back that turned all of a sudden, turned my world into darkness, where even shadows can't be made out because everything is so black you can't see a thing. And there are noises and you have to follow them but you don't know if it is your own heart forced to dance heavily to a wrong tune that makes it shatter and spit blood with every beat, or is it just the wind blowing down the alleys of some irrevocable truth that does not even exist outside its faithfulness.
        Am I dancing?
        Am I walking?
        Am I motionless?
        Do I speak?
        Do I listen?
        Do I care?

A: *in a corner of the room, looking up into the air, speaking to themself*
A castle in the sky...

J: *as if expecting an answer*
Why would I make up such a thing?

A: ...no inhabitants but the shapeless wind...

J: I'd dream about red rose romance if I was free to choose!

A: ...always blowing north...

J: But that's not me.
shaking their head, starting to move again

A: ...to greet his sisters in frozen springs...

J: No, that's not me. Maybe I wouldn't dream at all.

A: ...a never-ending melancholy ballet of lonely treetops...

J: This is no dream. This must be life.

A: ...where not even crows dare to settle...

J: This is no fantasy. This is real.

A: …as nothing's more fragile than a dream.

J: But what if I'm not?

Heartbeat goes on in the dark, finally slows down, stops.

IV

A: *standing, addressing Jamie as if having a sudden revelation*
       And time!

J: *sitting facing the audience, watching hands*
       It passes.

A: *stamps foot*
       No.

J: Yes.

A: Yes.
       That's not what I mean...

J: What do you mean?

A: Does it stop?

J: *shrugs*
       Sometime.

A: When?

J: *lying on back, hands 'dancing' above head*
            When we're dead.
            It dies with us.

A: But what if we don't die?

J: Everybody does.

A: But if we're asleep.

J: Then?

Alex lying down next to Jamie.

A: We will sleep forever.
            Time does not mean anything to those who dream.

J: So we're immortal. That's what you're saying.

A: That's what I'm saying.

J: That's it.

Silence.

A: Do you think it's true?

J: Depends.

A: On what?

J: If we're truly asleep...

A: Are we?

J: ...and we've been the whole time...

A: Were we?

J: We can't die!

A: We'll live forever.

J: Cause immortality means never being born at all.

Orchestral music.

V

A: *still lying on their back*
So we dream in a bubble of imagination that feeds us, that moves us, that is our supernatural womb, carrying us till we're old and wrinkled but we never age. We never had a mother. Who's the father to bodiless creation? It is warm and it is safe, it is cold and it is cruel, it is black and it is colourful. It's all. It's everything. There's nothing more. But I have a mother who is called Rachel and she has brown hair and wears trainers all the time even though she never leaves home.

fixing some point as if actually seeing their mother
This is my mother sitting behind her flowers and cactuses, for they are everywhere about the house especially since father left and never came back.

gets up, lots of gestures, talks very quickly, as if in fear, as if reliving everything
So I walk the streets that are rain washed and slippery, I won't be late, I said, and I turn left and cross the river and turn right and stand before a door. A black door that won't open, I knock till the skin on my fist is red and starts to bleed, only a bit, and I knock on and then I stop because I remember that I don't remember whose door it is I'm knocking at. And I don't know why I have to be here, but I have to be here, this is home, this is where all roads end, this is - and now the door opens...

J: *shouting madly*
Bang! BANG! BANG!

A: *startled*
Why you're screaming?

J: *shrugging*
I might wake up from the noise

A: I remember that noise.

J: *carefully*
Where did it come from?

A: A birch-trunk maybe.

J: A shell at some beach.

A: An old man losing his grip.

J: A town.

A: No town.

J: Everywhere.

A: Nowhere.

J: *facing Alex*
Shout at me!

A: No.

J: Shout at me!

A: No.

J: Why?
       taking Alex by their shoulders, shaking them
       Shout at me, shout at me, shout at me!

A: No! Why?

J: I can't wake myself up.

A: *shrugs*
       Neither can I.

J: *pleading*
       Shout at me.

A: NO!

J: C'mon, shout at me, please!

A: *yelling*
       FOR FUCK'S SAKE, LEAVE ME BE!

J: *calm again*
       You did it.

A: Sorry.

J: That's fine.

A: Did it work then?

J: I don't know.

A: Did it?

J: Nothing's changed.

A: It didn't.

J: I don't know.
       Maybe I've been awake already. How should you be
       able to wake me up if I've never been asleep in the first
       place?

A: Were you?

J: I don't know.

Pause, both in their own thoughts.

A: I'm not.

J: Asleep?

A: Can't tell.

J: You said -

A: Just know that I'm not.
        Asleep, awake, whatever.
        I'm just not.

Some seconds of music.

VI

Sitting next to each other facing the audience, each one following their own train of thoughts.

J: *resigned but decisive*
        I'd give half of my lifetime for some years by her side.

A: If I could master time, I would not be here...

J: I'd give half of my lifetime for some weeks with her.

A: I'd probably turn it back exactly to the point of my creation...

J: I'd give half of my lifetime to be with her for a few days.

A: and then I would make it stop and think about if what's happening is real...

J: I'd give half of my lifetime for a few hours by her side.

A: and if it was, I don't know if I would...

J: I'd give half of my lifetime to have her here now.

A: let it happen I don't know if...

J: But I've nothing to give. Time's not on my side.

A: I made it stop.

J: And life is running away from us.

A: I don't know if it really is.

Switching into a dialogue.

J: Something moves. And it's not us.

A: Not life, only time.

J: But life exists inside time.

A: But time only exists within ourselves.

J: They say time is a human construct.

A: So are we.

J: A construct cannot create another construct.

A: We're not moving.

J: We are moved.

A: By what?

J: I want to know why!

A: We're not real.

J: "...is all that we see or seem but a dream within a dream?"

A: *nodding in consent*
        all but a dream.

J: But then: who sleeps?

VII

Jamie barely visible in the back of the room, drawing a very large image of a woman's face onto the wall, absorbed, this goes on for a while, suddenly Alex starts, body restless, very emotional.

A: And he said stupid bitch and she said no, please, the kid, but he never stopped and I was hiding in the corner where the empty cans piled. And they were making little metallic noises because I was trembling and they shook with me as I tried to hold on to something comforting but only found cold bottles. Please, she said, but he was stronger, men always are, and I stopped looking. Now I know where I remember the noise from because it rang in my head when I closed my eyes 'cause I didn't want to see my mother being kicked in her stomach falling down when father was angry and blamed her for having lost his job and blamed her because he couldn't blame himself.

Stupid bitch, he said, don't cry mummy, I said, when he was gone and I held her in my arms, and then he was gone for good, she said that this was the best that ever happened to her and she started to collect plants as she didn't know what else she should do with her freedom.

muted

And as I went out the black door was closed as always but this time I didn't knock.

VIII

Music, still playing when they start to speak, but very softly.
They are sitting with their backs on opposing walls, in conversation,
normal voices, like old friends, exhausted.

J: Nobody ever said anything to me.

A: Who's nobody?

J: *turning towards drawing, staring at it with unveiled yearn-*
        ing and sadness
        It's her.

A: *gaping at it for a moment*
        Who's she?

J: Everything.

A: That's nothing.

J: That's all!

A: You can't say someone is everything 'cause they
        never can be, it's not possible, it's not. You know
        that the moment you say it and it's a lie, and a lie
        is a bad thing, especially if you like this person.
        You do like her?

J: *defeated*
        She's everything to me.

A: You can't say that.

J: *suddenly slightly angry*
        But I do because when she was there, I could feel it
        all, it was all there, and I can't even say what 'all'
        means but I know it must have been this way
        because when she was gone, I had nothing.

A: *sympathetic*
        Who is she?

J: *dazed*
        A dream that took shape.

A: You woke up?

J: All my life I had dreamed of her, I didn't know
        that, I only knew that I was not happy and there
        was something missing, but the moment I first
        saw her I knew that it was her, it's always been
        her.

A: So it was real?

J: *smiling in remembrance, beaming*
        And I managed to see her, I said, let me buy you a cof-
        fee, and she came with me and I told her all about

myself and she watched me with her crooked smile and sometimes she laughed out loud, I didn't know I was funny, guess I am, and when she laughed her whole body shook and her hair moved like a wild river of golden velvet and it sounded like cascading rippling of summer rain on the roof of a car.
smile slowly fades, pained expression

Each following their own train of thoughts.

A: *eyes closed*
        A rainbow splitting the day in two. On the right side, there only lies darkness.

J: And now sometimes I think while I was dreaming about her, my whole life about her, I was still awake and I just slipped into a dream when meeting her.
        on the verge of tears
        And when she rejected me I wished I would wake up, I prayed to God I would, but nothing happened.

A: *as if waking from a nightmare, checking walls, hands*
        There is blood on the walls, red and shiny, little dots on the floor. My hands are scarlet, but I remember nothing. Dripping scarlet, warm and sticky, I don't remember, but my hands are covered with blood.

J: *crying and bitter*
        And then I thought, I must be awake, I can't dream that, nobody dreams about their heart being crushed

(*spitting the words*) and shattered and emptied and battered and hurt and ripped apart and eaten and spit out and humiliated and diminished and bleeding and fading and blackening and shrinking and dead.

A: Maybe it was a nightmare.
        But my hands never got cleaner;
        rubbing hands
        I washed them for hours, till they were frozen and shaking from the cold water in the tap I spilt on my face. Still they were scarlet and the blood was still warm, and the stains never fade, I still wear them, but I can't see them.

J: And then I thought maybe we don't even dream ourselves, maybe we get dreamed by a god and that god must be cruel, cruel and careless.
        And maybe it's a nightmare and we can't wake because it's not us sleeping, it's not us.

A: *as if to persuade self, still rubbing hands*
        I'm not the creator of my life. Still I can change it.

J: I'm not the builder of my dreams. I can't change them.

A: *tearing at hands, burying head in them*
        Who says that nightmares can't come true?

VIII

First in front of drawing, then turns facing the audience.

J: And when I met her I said see, I have to protect you from the world and she just shook her head, didn't look at me once, just frowned and stayed silent. I need to protect you, I said and reached out
stretching out arm, unconsciously repeating other gestures as well
to touch a dark strain of her hair, no she breathed, her hair sadly dancing, embraced by air only, I need no protection, and she turned and started to walk away but I couldn't let her and I ran after her and reached for her and got hold of her hand so she looked at me and I died from green sadness as she said nothing but her eyes did, they did,
pauses
and I knew she didn't care for my protection and she wanted to be left alone and I died and she left and now I remember that this was the only time I touched her skin, but it was just a dream.
looking at empty hand

A: *crouched in some corner, voice of a preacher, mockingly*
Behold of the wolf that passes as a sheep...

J: And I wonder: did I ever meet her at all?

A: behold of the nightmare that dresses in dreams...

J: Did I talk to a wish that turned into a dream and faded into a nightmare 'cause reality couldn't host it?

A: behold of the extreme that never is real.

J: Maybe life can't be extended either way. It shrinks from desperation and hides from fulfilment. It's nothing but a dull base, like the bubble of a chewing gum bursting if its boundaries are stretched too far...
       Imitating exploding noise

A: exploding into nightmare at the low end...

J: and culminating into sunny dreams at the high.

A: But you can't remain on neither end.

J: No

A: There is no substance.

J: There is no flesh.

A: Our emptied bodies long for accomplice in the flesh.

J: Our uprooted minds long for comfort in dreams.

A: Which way to turn?

J: Which road to choose?

A: Which path to thread?

J: It's all wrong.

A: Nothing holds it all.

J: It's all wrong.

A: Nothing holds us all.

J: We're all wrong.

IX

A: *sitting on the ground, franticly drawing a circle with one finger again and again*
I was standing in front of the black door, again I knocked, as always, I knocked till my knuckles hurt, and when the paint came down, black rain cutting my eyes, I saw that I had knocked a hole in the wood, black rain still, maybe the size of a fingernail, black, and I looked at the hole and through and it was red, flames of red, scarlet fire. And the hole fits the stain, the crumbled blood on my hand.
looks at own hand

J: Once I thought about killing myself.

A: It's not a black door, never was.

J: *makes a fist*
Killing...

A: It's a red door.

J: *bangs fist against drawing*
her...

A: I painted it black.

J: pride.
        When she left.
        Now caressing the drawing

A: Scarlet.
        I.
        died.
        It.

J: *resigned*
        I thought about killing.

Both as if telling a story to the audience, unconsciously complement-
ing each other.

A: And once I knew the door was not black I couldn't
        knock anymore.

J: But I couldn't.

A: I tried very hard, but I couldn't.

J: Her departure just an illusion...

A: My hand just wouldn't move.

J: as she never arrived...

A: paralyzed I stood...

J: at my doorstep.

A: I stand.

J: Never will.

A: Always.

X

Both very emotional, broken, unaware of each other until the end when they enter dialogue again.

A: I hate him but I wish he'd come back, I wish he'd come back.

J: She never will. She never was there.

A: *tearing at own shoelaces*
        Once she told me why she was wearing shoes all the time, even in bed, it's because of him, she said. If he'll come back I'm gonna have to run, I want to be prepared for that, I'm gonna have to run.

J: And her eyes were as cold and gleaming as the icy top of a mountain but around the pupil, there was a ring of deep silver and I felt that it was a hidden treasure I had to seek out, but I didn't and when she turned away I only saw the reflection of my tears in that silver and I never cried, I couldn't.

fists into eyes

A: He's never coming back, I saw it on the news, he got hit by a car, I know it was him, downtown. Noises of rush-hour traffic, breaks screeching, shouting
They said his name, because he was a well-known someone once, they said his name and that he was drunk. His last words were I'm gonna kill that bitch and of course he can't, he got killed himself, but mum must have seen it, too and now she's afraid of ghosts.

J: And her ghost is still haunting me, day after day, and it will always be there and she never will be but I will be haunted by that shadow of hers till the end of my time because I can't live without her.

A: I wish he would come back so I can kill him.

J: She'd just reject me.

A: I wish he would come back so I can kill him again.

J: Irrevocably unrequited whish, out of reach. My hands only grasping air, grasping the splinters of something that once was or never was, cutting through me like I was nothing.
pause, then as if having found a solution
It's because I sleep, I can't be anything while being asleep.

A: Who knows? Maybe the sleeping meet the dead, maybe it's possible, maybe it's all possible.

J: It is.

A: It is. The only thing impossible to know is to know.

J: Someone knows.

A: Who knows?

J: *shrugging*
Someone.

A: Maybe we know.

J: We can't know.

A: We don't want to know.

J: Maybe.

A: We shouldn't know.

Both slowly go back to initial position from Scene I, but stare intently into the eyes of the spectators for a while. When the audience gets uneasy, they speak again.

J: Someone knows.

A: We don't.

J: We don't.

A: Someone does.

J: Someone.

A: But we can't trust.

J: No, we can't trust.

A: No.

Immediate black.
Music from the beginning, again very loud.